1

PRODUCTIVITY

The foundation.

Graeme Smith

PUBLISHED ON AMAZON.com
by
LABYRINTH BOOKS

DEDICATION

This book is dedicated to my family.

Hele-ly (Ly).
my wife:

Ingrid.
our daughter:

Marie.
my former wife:

Fiona, Natalie and Michael
our children:

Georgie
Michael's wife:

Pearl, Kiki and Martha.
their children:

They have put up with me for many years and I thank them for that.
I hope this book gives them an insight into what has occupied me.
Well for much of the time.
They have all done worthwhile and interesting things.
Without much help from me.
I congratulate them for their achievements.

AN ART CAREER STARTED LIKE THIS.
1. The nature of art was considered
2. Related to these aims, are more specific objectives.
3. That's what SPACE Art Education stands for!
4. SPACE Art Education makes these assumptions.

1. The nature of art was considered.

The following are AIMS derived from this analysis.

To develop the uniqueness of each student.

To develop confident self-actualization.

To develop self-responsibility and initiative.

To develop creativity and flexibility of thinking.

To develop visual perceptual ability.

In relation to the individual learner they develop these qualities:

Unique person

Self-actualization

Self-responsibility

Creativity

Perceptual skills

An Art Career assumes creativity is a behaviour all have.

Even without any teaching.

Suitable educational methods can develop higher skill levels.

The value of appropriate behaviour is stressed.

An interaction of perception, affect and cognition is creativity.

An Art Career provides appropriate strategies.

They expose students to the creative process.

Nurture their creative response.

And develop creativity skill as a consequence.

Planned, deliberate, sequenced and non-verbal strategies.

The diagram illustrates the various OBJECTIVES and their relationship to coach strategies and student LEARNING EXPERIENCES.

2. Related to the aims are more specific objectives.

Skills attitudes and concepts are integrated and developed.
Thus later stages incorporate earlier ones.
Creativity is the behaviour intrinsic to both art and education.

STIMULUS Structured	SKILLS Perceptual	ATTITUDES Affective	CONCEPTS Cognitive	LEARNING Experiences
Concrete	Visual Tactual Manipulative	Receiving Responding	Evaluation	Awareness
Sensory		Valuing	Synthesis	Expressive Analysis
Verbal			Organization Application	Experimental Comprehensive
Personal		Value Complex	Knowledge	Existential

3. That's what SPACE Art Education stands for!

Structured STIMULUS – a planned and organized program.
Perceptual SKILLS – student develop in response to a stimulus.
Affective ATTITUDES – emotion guides student options.
Cognitive CONCEPTS – creative thinking determines the action.
Experiences LEARNING – which is how learning happens.

4. Like SPACE Art Education,

COACH CREATIVITY SKILL makes these assumptions:

1. The core of creativity is interaction of feeling, thinking and doing.
2. Each learning experience should be enjoyable but serious.
3. This is primarily a time for student action rather than coach talk.
4. The learning experience is seen by the student as self-rewarding.
5. Each student works independently.

HOW TO USE THIS BOOK.

Usually people don't think through things to the level they need to.
Because of that, they have projects instead of tasks on their "to do" list.
That leads to procrastination for it hasn't been broken down to a task level.
So go through your book once to understand it THEN go through it again.

Then start at the BEGINNING.
Make notes of the steps you will need to take and the resources required.
Use notes to create a step by step system for implementing particular ideas.
Often you won't refer back to an original, once you've created **YOUR** system.

The first question to ask and answer is "Why is this being done?"
How does this align with where you want to get to?
What are the strategic implications of doing this?
Does this fit in with getting to a goal in the shortest and fastest time?
What would it be like if it were totally successful?
Define it - what is success for this project and how will you know?

Now brainstorm all the tasks are involved in your project.
It's important not to go linear too fast with this.
By linear, I mean step one, step two, step three, and step four.
You end up cutting off options.
As you plan step one, two, three, there is a specific step that might be four.
Start steps too quickly, other ways for one, two and three may not appear.

The first third of a brainstorming session is easy - find lots of ideas.
The second third is challenging – look at the ideas to see where they go.
Then push to think a bit outside the box for that's often where the big idea is!
That's where the most powerful way of getting a project done the fastest - is.

Most never get to that level and end up short-changing themselves.
Then their project takes longer and they also set up to procrastinate.
This final brainstorming part of the equation is incredibly important.

Once you've brainstormed a project put options into a linear sequence.
Then you can figure out what you've overlooked and all becomes obvious.
Get tasks in order, add missing steps, and lay out your list for the project.

Once you've organized the tasks into a linear process decide:
What things can you start immediately?
What can start that is not dependent on things that must occur beforehand?
There might be five, six or twenty that don't rely on anything else to happen.
You can get started on them right away!

Write things you think of and cross off things as you do them.
Add in stuff that is relevant from time to time.

MY FOCUS.

I have taken many years to learn lessons and develop materials.
You are welcome to look elsewhere but will not find solutions such as I offer.
Some may even sound similar but they WILL be different.
I doubt if others have the individual components nor philosophical orientation.

ART
What is essential for art to exist?
There **IS** an answer and it is the foundation of An Art Career.

Whatever art is MUST happen every time art happens!
If Art = x then x must happen whenever art happens.
Not sometimes, occasionally or even mostly BUT - **ALWAYS**.

So what is art?
Art **IS** creativity expressed using visual material.
That is **ALL** art, of any kind, of any standard.
It is an action – something that is done.

CAREER
What values does art have when placed in a commercial context.
All things done in a commercial context are done for business reasons.
Otherwise they are optional.

Is there something about art that can also commercial?
If people pay money there should be some benefit for them.
That should be the focus of an art business program and is of An Art Career.

An Art Career is not rocket science but common sense.
It is art business for the 21st Century brought right up to date in this book.

But it has also been tested in real life.
An Art Career works because it is right.
The thinking and the practice are in harmony.

THE REAL TEST

The success of a professional career is measured by money earned.

Income is the **ONLY** objective way to measure your professional success.

BUT it's not me that will build your art business for you.

You are the professional artist running your business.

To get **ANY** benefit you must actually **DO** something!

There is very little benefit gained by merely reading my material.

PRODUCTIVITY: A FOUNDATION.

SUPPORT:

The Australian Artist magazine – magazine for artists

The International Artist magazine – magazine for artists

Clipping Path Universe – for photo-shop editing

Cherri Computers –computer hardware, software and printers

1. Productivity - the seed.

Reviewed by Kathy Kay-Voysey - (Mudgee, Australia)

1. Productivity – The foundation of a professional career.

When I run this course with REAL LIVE students I start a bit differently.
The main thing I do differently is the first thing is give them an experience.
This is similar to the one I have written for you to do.
BUT there is a major difference so I have a problem.

I ALWAYS start by providing a practical experience for my students.
They have to use paint, paper and probably a brush.
That's the FIRST thing they get.

I do this in EXACTLY the SAME way that I have set out for you.
But they do NOT get a chance to read anything first like you had.

At each step they do NOT know what (if anything) is coming next.
I tried to find a way of exposing you to EXACTLY the same experience.
BUT unfortunately it is NOT the same.
You can read the lot and anticipate what is about to happen next.

My students do NOT know what I am about to do.
They cannot anticipate materials to be used, nor order they are issued in.
Thus they have to use what they have at any time as best they can.

You can read everything and then do what I suggest.
You can even read everything and then NOT do anything at all.
Either way it is then it is too late.
You can no longer have the same kind of experience real live students had.
BUT that's what I want to provide.

Someone providing a similar experience can overcome the problem.
They CAN vary the actual materials or their quantity or sequence of issue.
From this beginning is possible to grow creativity skill in any group over time.

But first the seed needs to be planted!
Special instructions are opened as each part of the planting is completed.

EACH SPECIAL INSTRUCTION STARTS LIKE THIS!

YOU WILL FIND THIS AT THE END OF EACH SPECIAL INSTRUCTION.

Do NOT go to the next page.
Only if you have carried out the SPECIAL INSTRUCTION on this page!
So after you have carefully read this page then go to the next page.
But NOT before that!
EVENTUALLY THE SEED IS SOWN AND GERMINATION BEGINS.

2. The FIRST special instruction!

Get these materials so you can plant the seed.

A large piece of cardboard, a brush, a white paper rectangle (25cmx15cm).

Also several pieces of coloured wool.

And RED, BLUE, YELLOW, WHITE and BLACK paint.

There is NO need to use expensive paints.

Use these materials only when given a specific instruction to do so.

Are the right materials available?

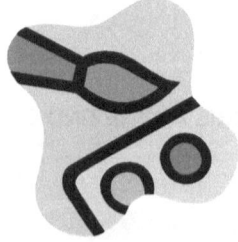

Do NOT go to the next page.

Only if you have carried out the SPECIAL INSTRUCTION on this page!

When you have those materials then you can go to the next page.

But NOT until then!

3. The SECOND special instruction is next!

Have these materials ready to use.

A brush.

A piece of white paper about 25cm x 15cm.

A large piece of cardboard to keep your desk or table clean.

Squeeze a thin circle of yellow paint onto your paper, just like icing a cake.

Do not use any of the other materials at this stage.

Please do those things?

Do NOT go to the next page.

Until you have carried out the SPECIAL INSTRUCTION on this page!

When those materials are ready, go to the next page but NOT until then!

4. The THIRD special instruction!

Decide what to do - explore, find out what you can do.
Start when you like (quickly or slowly).

This is an experiment (like in Science).
Find out whatever you can.
Work without interference from anyone else.
Probably there is no-one else present anyway.

Later you will use more things.
That will be after you run out of yellow.
Do not take more before that happens.

When you have done all you can - wait - can you do more?

Go to the next page if you have carried out this SPECIAL INSTRUCTION!

5. The FOURTH special instruction follows!

Do all you can with the yellow!

Then put a blob of red paint on your cardboard backing.
The red paint is **NOT** placed on the painted paper.

The blob of paint should be very SMALL - a small coin is big enough.
Do not use any of the other materials yet.
So please do those things?

When you have the second material (red paint) continue.
Start again when you are ready - just do what you can with the red paint.

Do not hurry this process - wait.
Take your time --- do not hurry.

Carry out the SPECIAL INSTRUCTION on this page THEN:
After you have used the red paint you can go to the next page.
But NOT until then!

6. The FIFTH special instruction is now!

After you have done all you can do
Repeat the previous step but with a length of coloured wool.
Use the wool and the sheet of painted white paper.
Do NOT use any other materials.

Wait.
You could use more wool if you like.

Do NOT go to the next page.
Only if you have carried out the SPECIAL INSTRUCTION on this page!
When you have used the strip of paper then go to the next page.
But NOT until then!

7. The SIXTH and LAST special instruction!

When you have done all you can:
Place a blob of white paint on the art board.
Continue when you are ready.
Just do what you can with the white paint.
The white paint is the last thing so then you will finish.

You decide whether to keep or discard your experiment.
When you have done all you can do and are finished.

Put away the piece of cardboard and the brush.
Everything should now be clean.

An experiment may take 15 minutes.
Particularly if you go VERY slowly.
Do NOT hurry for time is an important ingredient in an experiment.

That was the last SPECIAL INSTRUCTION.
You can go to the next page whenever you like.

2. IMPROVING PRODUCTIVITY.

Reviewed by Geoff Fellows - (Wagga Wagga, Australia.)

1. Do you have what it takes?
2. Quantity is the key to guaranteed quality.
3. Once I tested an art education program.
4. Skill comes from practice.
5. Paint in your own style.
6. Eliminate wasted time.
7. Getting a career started?

1. Do you have what it takes?

You may even be able to paint well.
But let's be frank, painting well is nowhere near enough.
Many failed professional artists paint as well as any successful one.
Also there are successful professional artists who do not paint well at all.
Painting ability will NOT decide if you are successful as a professional artist.

Money is a totally objective measure of success!
It doesn't matter what kind of art you do.

It may take 3 to 5 years for you to hit the jackpot, but so what?
A six-figure income in 3 to 5 years as a professional artist is a great goal.
It's also reasonable if you're prepared to learn, and maintain your focus.
BUT you must also WORK!

No-one can start a career, or continue in it, without capital backing.
This must be either your own, or from other sources.
Depending on sales is NOT sufficient!

Advanced strategies which can grow your wealth will NOT work.
UNTIL you've laid a solid foundation for your career.

Successful professional artists work hard!
Successful professional artists typically love their career.

Too many artists aren't prepared to do the work!
What sacrifices will YOU make to enjoy a successful professional career?
Have you really got the stamina and drive it takes to create **lasting** success?

2. Quantity is the key to guaranteed quality.

As a professional you need to paint more in less time!
BUT you may find that your standard is not what it was and selling is harder.

Small sizes avoid any preciousness attached to the result.
So just do something – anything – but keep it small.

Experiment rather than producing a finished painting.
Keep your experiments to about 25cm x 15cm or less.

Just paint anything in any way and it's a powerful tool.
Make 5 or 10 or 20 experiments a part of your daily routine.

Small sizes speed up production of those experiments.
There is more time on a large area than a small one, no matter what image.
Decreasing the size of your work can increase productivity dramatically.
Most may not even be finished and DON'T frame them.
Because they aren't to be framed or sold it will not matter how they turn out.

Avoid major (big) works though.
They take time, are usually done slowly and are often large and complex.
You'll tend to labour over them as you seek to do your best.
High school and college art classes have much to answer for here!

It doesn't matter what you do at the start, as long as you do something.
It can be random but you do not need that, then develop what you have
Imagination cannot work on a blank surface, it needs help!
You don't have to wait for inspiration - make a few marks.
That's all your mind needs!

3. Once I tested an art education program.

The teaching was closely linked to the materials issued to the pupils.
The particular material combinations were NOT random.
The challenge was to see what could be created with any given combination.

One teacher over a series of these lessons noticed a particular boy.
In the earliest lessons there were always two blobs present in the work.
It didn't matter what he was given by the teacher.

Over a period of time the two blobs gradually changed into birds.
They were just basic symbol-type birds, such as most people might do.

As the lessons continued the birds improved.
Eventually they became recognizable as budgerigars.
The teacher realized the boy made budgerigars irrespective of materials.

The boy became a challenge for the teacher.
He tried to find a combination of materials that couldn't become budgerigars.
The boy always found ways - once he pin-pricked budgerigars in paper.
What chance this kid might become the best budgerigar artist in the world?
If he continued, I'd say every chance.

Why did he do this?
Well the teacher discovered (surprise) he had two pet budgerigars.
They meant more to this boy than anything else.
The boy expressed his feelings and knowledge as he wasn't told what to do.

Like the boy you should paint something you want to paint.
There is an idea you want to develop OR something you want to try.
That's what having sincerity and integrity is about!
Any other reason and it will be hard to maintain motivation and enthusiasm.
Particularly in the long term (as a professional career will be).

With experiments do stuff you want to paint, or ideas you have in mind.
That's how it should be to paint the human figure, if that's what you want.
For a portrait artist all experiments could be people, hands, faces or noses.
Just do them and they'll improve provided the motivation is strong enough.

Your experiments are mainly to develop your ability and attitude.
If you work quickly productivity also improves as you work faster and better.

If there is no challenge, then there is no reason for painting.
It's an exercise and will tend to become repetitious and eventually boring.

4. Skill comes from practice.

Paint hundreds of small experiments.
The quality will improve, particularly if you don't worry about it when painting.
It takes some time before you notice the improvement, but it will happen!
Naturally this improvement will not be at the start.

At the very least you will learn what not to do and what won't work.
That knowledge takes you closer to what will work and what should be done.

Forget about standards for that is a barrier to finding your own way.
Look back from time to time and see if you have improved.
You'll get a pleasant surprise as you've consistently lifted the bar higher.

What will become of all those experiments?
A professional artist needs a detached view of their own works!
Here's where you can start developing that!

A professional artist knows they must part with most of their best work.
You'll eventually accept this as part of being a professional artist.

You can do that because you'll know there WILL be more 'best' ones.
Thus you'll be less worried than the beginner who fears that there will not be.
Your many experiments will help you realize the truth of this.

You also commit ideas to your memory bank which are accessible later.
Looking at various experiments refreshes your ideas beyond those recorded.
Just don't think standard while you paint.
The more you do, the better you get, and the higher your standard becomes.

Let's say you want to learn to paint the human figure?
Then do figures – lots of them but do not worry about how they turn out.
Just paint them and in time they'll improve.

You might feel anxious about this approach.
There's nothing to be anxious about as the results simply do not matter.

They are not for sale, not for show, not for framing.
They are simply experiments to explore your thoughts.

Often artists are too careful?
They are frightened of making a mistake.
If you fear mistakes you'll never learn anything, only repeat what you know.
Just get on and do them without worrying about how they turn out.

You learn to paint by painting.
Exhibitions where all the works look similar demonstrate the artist's style.
Exhibitions which look like several different artists painted the works.
Show a lack of style but possibly a mastery of skill.

5. Paint in your own style.

Remember it's quantity that counts.
That's why small is best for then you can do most.

Similarly acrylic is quicker than oils but can look like oils.
For more texture use impasto mediums or mix a binder with the paint.

You may decide to return to your current medium at a later date.
Then you have new insights gained from this experience.
But at least there's a choice!

You may not want to make this change.
BUT you never really know what a difference using acrylic paint could make.
It can influence your productivity, income and probably style as well!

I'm vague about measurements because the exact size doesn't matter.
As long as it's small – say between 10cm x 10cm and 30cm x 30cm.
BUT they don't have to be squares or even all the same size.

They don't have to be on canvas either.
You could easily use brown paper, cardboard or whatever is available,
If you fancy being a watercolourist, then by all means use watercolour paper.
BUT try various grades just to discover the differences that happen.

Quantity is the key to improvement.
Painting a large number of experiments will develop painting skills/
Also attitude - you'll become more discerning as you gain more experience.
You'll not need, nor want, other people's assessments.

The whole approach is experimental.
Explore and discover what can be done in any medium.
Use whatever support you like.
Although you probably use the same regularly.
Because that's what you like and understand.

As you get better you'll get even quicker!
People who do anything well also do it faster than those who don't.
That applies to painting as much as anything else for it's an indicators of skill.

Skill in art, sport or medicine is basically the same phenomenon.
It's practiced behaviour in action.
Most artists don't do anywhere near enough paintings to develop real skill.
That why your experiments should be an important part of a daily routine.

6. Eliminate wasted time.

Work on a number of paintings at the same time.
Once you run into a dead-end with a painting go to another for a fresh start.
Eventually the first painting has a different attitude or set aside again.

Can't remember what you did previously - do what you think of now.
In the end it doesn't matter as most works finish roughly at the same time.

Use larger brushes
Another way to speed up your painting is to use larger brushes.
Try various brushes and see how large a brush you can use.

House painting brushes can be used instead of artists' brushes.
With practice you can paint the majority of any painting with a large brush.
If necessary, finer brushes can be used to finish off the work.

Don't worry about having proper stretchers and all the best materials.
That puts pressure on - save that for when your art career really gets going.
Even paint on paper or cardboard it simply won't matter what you paint on!

When you buy paint, buy in quantity, but only use as needed.
A particular colour can be applied to the work for which it was intended.
BUT there are usually other works where that same colour is appropriate.

Let your works evolve.
Your exercises are pre-season training with the main game yet to come!

Later there will be major works of a standard you are proud of.
Right now we are looking for improvement and consistency.

Eventually some will be larger than others, but all will be your best!
You are the judge of quality, which is a variable that changes over time.
You must have old works you thought were excellent when they were done.
What are they like now?

Not all of the exercises will turn out perfectly.
But that won't matter because you'll learn a great deal from the 'failures'.
You'll learn what to do and what not to do next time.

You do not need a big space either.
Just stack the finished experiments against a wall.
They could be on top of one another, even throw them out as they're done!

7. Getting a career started?

At this stage don't be concerned with sales for that puts pressure on.
You become careful which slows the process down.

BUT work to will increase your chances of financial success later.
You are learning rather than earning (that will come)!

People pay more for oils or anything that looks like oils.
If you want to earn money and be a professional that's the way to go!
A watercolour style can be used, but with acrylic on canvas or a board.

BUT you will find acrylic is better than oil.
That's because you paint faster and make more paintings in the same time.

Productivity is directly correlated with potential earnings.
Eventually there's less framing expense too because there's no glass.

Works under glass have been cheapened by the flood of prints.
As a result watercolourists have a much harder job making a living.
That medium and also pastel has a lower image and lower prices follow.
Why practice with stuff costs more to frame, harder to sell and returns less?

In your studio you don't have to clean up and can leave stuff around.
You can't be a professional artist without this so claim a space.
Paint in a studio, sell in the marketplace, different important environments.

Many artists see a gallery exhibition the start of a professional career!
It might be too IF you have the foundation for a professional career in place.

But why would you plan this step!
Is it because you'd like an exhibition, and you need a gallery to do this?
That's the least likely reason to lead to a satisfactory outcome.

Galleries are to make money for its owner and artists who exhibit there.
Holding exhibitions is one way this is done.
Galleries are not usually in business to provide artists with exhibition spaces.
Particularly if they feel like having an exhibition just to show their work!

It's better to take another year or two and start then from strength.
Commence exhibiting prematurely and after that play a catch-up game.
But you won't catch up because gallery visitors have long memories.
Their first impressions will be the ones that are strongest.

Those impressions will NOT be of your works but of a failed exhibition.
Those memories stay with them, no matter what you do, even years later.
An experienced gallery owner will reject you if they think this is possible.

But should you even be talking to them at this stage?
To make sure you know what you're in for talk to your accountant first.
If you don't have one, find one, their advice is needed regularly.
You'll also need a lawyer/ solicitor, but not as often.

Contact anyone else who helps people start their own careers.
Depending where you live this could be the Chamber of Commerce,
Department of Consumer Affairs, Department of Small Business or bank.

Select advisors who are experienced helping people start a career.
Cheapest is not always best so use accountants and solicitors sensibly.
If they've assisted people in the art industry, great but they'll be hard to find.

Another group of advisers will be those already in the art industry.
Other artists and galleries provide advice freely, particularly on starting.
Add their advice to the career advice.
Don't accept everything as truth for many myths are perpetuated this way.

You'll now realize a professional artist doesn't just produce paintings.
Sell, market, keep accounts, finance and tasks all small business people do.
You could be frightened at the money you must earn each and every year.

Amateur artists don't need to do these things, a professional must.
It's the amateur or hobby artist who can just spend their time painting.
You have to run you small business (being a professional artist) as well.
But you still must paint too or there's nothing to sell!

3. PRODUCTIVITY TOOLS.

Reviewed by Dawn Lewis - (Clearwater, Florida.)

1. Write, illustrate, record ideas about your career and business.
2. Start a diary.
3. Start a success diary.
4. Buy a blank yearly planner at an office supplies store.

1. Write, illustrate, record ideas about your career and business.

Writing down thoughts is very powerful.
Commit those thoughts to your memory bank so they are accessible later.

Do this regularly, even daily.
Record answers to tasks and question from this book.
But do not limit yourself to only using the book for that.
Look at various pages in your Ideas Book later will refresh the ideas.
You will remember more than what is merely recorded in your book.

Use the Ideas Book to plan effectively.
Effective planning is the beginnings of effective actions.
Your plans are the test runs for the real world.
Plans by themselves don't make anything happen, but they ease the way.

Get the most from your Ideas Book.
Write stuff down.
Actually carry out some ideas.
Take your time.
Stick to the basics.
Theory and practice go together so review aspects that give problems.

2. Start a diary.

Record dates and times of scheduled events.

Carry it with you and also keep it near your phone.

Update it each day before you leave your studio.

Also record events that have gone.

This may be by making additional notes to a reminder entry.

3. Start a success diary.

If you're already keeping an Ideas Book, that will do.
Any time you have done something well (not necessarily perfectly).
Put the entries in a coloured ink or different coloured font or highlight them.

Note any progress on any project you've been procrastinating on.
When you do something for the first time or step outside your comfort zone.

Do any of these, record it and congratulate yourself in the diary.
The longer you do that, the more confidence you will build.
Constantly remind yourself that you're better than you give yourself credit for.
Recall times and places where you've had specific successes in the past.
It doesn't matter whether it's related to your art career or not.
They could also be education; family, hobbies, sport, or learning new things.

List successes so you can quickly review them from time to time.
Most people experience more success than we can call to mind at any time.
When you're feeling like a failure, you usually can't recall past successes!
They can be powerful concrete reminders of what you are capable of doing.
There are memories you carry around with you like emotional baggage.
Usually they're memories from your past when things didn't go right!
You can consciously decide they don't mean what you originally gave them.
A meaning that could be now damaging your confidence in yourself.

So start building self-confidence with your memories.
A basic example of this is reframing a failure as a learning opportunity.
The painting was not a success but you learned how to start any painting.
Reframing past failure can clear memories that erode confidence.
But it's not easy.

Doubts cost you more than you realize, they also cost performance.
They cost the ability for others to believe in, work with and help you succeed.
They cost you in your willingness to jump in and get things done.

Make it a habit to do something each day you would prefer not to do.
It might be picking up a phone and having a hard conversation.
It might be taking an action with your career that you've been putting off.
Or shutting the internet for an hour a day to focus on something important.
Something that - left to your own devices - you probably wouldn't do.

4. Buy a blank yearly planner at an office supplies store.

Enter dates of exhibitions, deliveries, works sold, and other key dates.
Then all can be seen at a glance **IF** you keep your Yearly Planner up to date.

Check it regularly to add new events, mark those no longer relevant etc.
Eventually all from start of a year until the end is on your Yearly Planner.
Keep your Yearly Planner fixed to a wall where it is easily seen.

Do not take it down when you add the next one.
Then you have reminders of past events which may happen again.

4: DEVELOP A LONG-TERM FOCUS.

Reviewed by Delores Eckberg – (Black Hawk, South Dakota)

1. Most people give urgent matters a priority.
2. Have you said things like?
3. Key decisions to design an effective system:
4. The first draft of a system is usually less than perfect:
5. Excellence is not attained but something you strive for.
6. The toughest part is actually deciding what to do FIRST.
7. Just how serious are you?

1. Most people give urgent matters a priority.

But there is NO long-term view.
It helps to keep a focus simple so you are not easily side-tracked.
More ideas don't produce an outstanding focus but fewer and better ones!

Instead make your focus easy to be remembered!
An important aspect is uniqueness at the time you first claim the focus.
What you say about yourself has to be different from what other artists say.
Audacity, even shock, can help make a focus memorable.

Repetition is a powerful force.
The more often the focus is repeated, the stronger it becomes.
An upward spiral of dominance results from repetition, and thus momentum.

A focus is powerful when it attracts the right clients'
It's the belief in your client's mind that you will be a great success.
A healthy career is narrowly focused with a dominant market share.
Such a career gives healthy profits and is almost impervious to competition.

A narrower product line can mean lower returns, INITIALLY.
It may be hard to appreciate but ultimately there's increased market share.
It's like pruning a plant, do it you end up with a better and healthier plant!

It's easy to lose direction though.
Artists are very likely to diversify in the present tough economic times.
BUT you lose focus and strength, particularly against others who keep focus.
You might feel you can't progress but it is how artists lose career momentum!

Artists are likely to diversify in present tough economic times.
You lose focus and strength, particularly against opposition who retain theirs.

It's better to look for an increase in the business you already have.
That way you'll increase your market power.
It's easier to increase your share in a career you know, than one you don't!

Let's say a popular local artist decides to expand by painting flowers.
They certainly know their own art (landscapes) very well.
They are likely to feel they can't make any more expansion in that area.

But they are confident about an area of career they DON'T know.
They have no experience at painting and selling floral artworks!

This is one of the main ways an artist loses career momentum!
They spend their time on something they don't know instead of what they do!

It's better to ask if a given decision will improve your career focus.
How can your present focus become a narrower range of works not more?

It may take a while for people to adjust to your refined focus.
So INITIALLY there could be a reduction in sales.
However ultimately there'll be an increase in market share.

A healthy career is narrowly focused with a dominant market share.
Such a career produces good profits and is almost impervious to competition.
You need to restrict growth which is similar to pruning a plant.
If you do it you end up with a better and healthier plant – well career!

What is your focus now?

2. Have you said things like?

I need to make more money ...
Or I wish I could work less and make more...
Or my career is consuming my life ...
Or I have almost no free time...
Or I wish I could spend less time putting out fires ...
Instead of spending more time growing my career!

These are easy to fix for they are from a career without systems.
A career that's fully dependent on one person - **YOU** - for everything.

Identify which areas to systemize?
Then you'll be free to enjoy your life and can do whatever you want to do.
Organizing and systemizing your entire career may seem like a major task.
But it only requires a small time commitment for just a few weeks.

Once you begin systemizing your career you'll free up lots of time.
So invest one to three hours a week to begin systemizing your career.
Shortly you free up more time than the initial commitment to systemizing.

Identify the tasks to systemize and keep a list called your "Fix-It List."
Write down all that goes wrong with your career that needs to be fixed.
An un-systemized career has problems all the time so keep the list handy.
It's important to write them down as they occur so you don't forget them.

Your Fix-It List is the start your systemizing efforts.
Initially eliminate the consistent problems in your career.

Now create these lists to highlight the career areas to systemize:
The most time-consuming tasks
The most stressful tasks
The most profitable tasks
The most important tasks

Try to come up with at least 10 items for each of those lists.
From the lists choose the tasks and procedures you want to systemize first.
Start with the most important parts of your career.
To determine which one to start with, ask yourself this question:
Which problem or challenge if eliminated.
Will reduce the most problems, free up most time, and make most money?

Now determine who is going to create the system
You work for yourself so YOU will have to design the system!
But let's say you want to systemize an agent's task.
The agent is responsible for the documentation for creating the system.
Record the steps, standards, and guidelines.
But first, decide on all the key elements of your new system.

3. Key decisions to design an effective system:

Who should perform this procedure?
If you don't define who is responsible for a procedure, you're responsible!
You want to assign procedures to specific roles, not to specific individuals.
The system should be executed by the sales staff, not Sally.

Over time all responsibilities documented for each specific role.
If a person leaves you don't change your policy and procedure manual.
If several members are needed it's important to list all their roles as well.
Every member of a team is aware of what every other member does.

What results should this procedure produce?
Specific, measurable results make your entire career predictable.

The only way is if you make your expectations clear.
Then design systems to achieve them.

When should the work be done?
Timing and frequency of when a procedure is to be done is often missing.
Is this procedure done daily - three times a week or every Monday?
The first day of the month, or the procedure is done haphazardly or not at all.

Why is the work important?
Your team members need to know why something is important.
Other people often see only their work process.
They don't know how their work fits into the big picture.
This makes it difficult to optimize your team's performance.

How should the procedure be completed?
This step is what most people think of when they think about systemizing.
The procedure is documented in a "step-by-step" manner.

No matter who does the work they do it the same way each time.
And, more importantly, generate the same results each time, too.

Record the steps on a piece of paper as you do them.
If you already do the activity, the easiest way to record the process is to do it.

Document your new system.
Identify all of the system's key elements.
This can include checklists, details, pictures, diagrams, and videos.

Make procedures identical in presentation.
Then their individual instructions will come through loud and clear.

That's why after each system is created and drafted.
Standardize procedures into a formal document for distribution.
And put it into your procedure manuals.

Identify everything with digital pictures, checklists, arrows, diagrams.
They should define exactly how each procedure is to be accomplished.
Or what the end result should look like.

4. The first draft of a system is usually less than perfect:

So test and tweak
Once a new system is documented it needs to be tested.
Whoever developed the system follows the steps to see what needs fixing.
If anything needs tweaking, he or she can make the necessary corrections.

Give the documented system to someone else.
This person should have less knowledge than the system's creator.
Find out if someone unfamiliar with a procedure can easily follow the system.
This is normally where glitches will surface.
Any issues should be sent back to the creator for revision.

Repeat until someone not a system creator easily executes the system.
Now a system has been tested there's one final step before it gets rolled out.
As owner, you sign off new procedures incorporated into your career.
Make sure each system is consistent with your overall vision and values.

Now it's time to give it to anyone responsible for executing it.
Train them in executing it exactly as it's laid out.
Insist everyone do it to your career standard - no exceptions, including you.
If anyone protests or has a better idea, put it back on "Fix-It List" for revision.

You should revisit your systems every six months.
Then you can ensure that they are being used properly and are working well.

Are people following the systems exactly as they are documented?
People will not always want to follow the systems.
Over time they revert to doing things their own way instead of your way.
Don't let them.

As you have more systems and people to use them your job changes.
You'll transform from doer to coach.
You will go from controller of the work to manager of the systems.

Don't make a bureaucracy!
With procedures for random or infrequent problems.
Or problems that have little chance of resurfacing.
You don't want to create systems for insignificant activities either.
This creates unnecessary complexity due to the sheer volume of information.

A guideline is only create systems you're willing to continually enforce.
Only create systems you want executed exactly the same way every time.
If it's not that important, then don't waste the time creating a system for it.

What about a system to create systems?
Create the precise instructions for creating systems in your career.
That way, you don't have to be the only one creating them.
The outline is for several hundred systems necessary for your operation.
This document ensures that each system shares the same tone and format.

Modify and personalize the steps suggested and make them your own.
Detail exactly the steps that every system will go through from inception.

5. Excellence is not attained but something you strive for.

Continually improve as nothing ventured, nothing gained is true.
Whatever happens because you take risks, you will not fail!

At the very least you will learn what not to do and what won't work.
That knowledge takes you closer to what will work and what should be done.
All major advances come from this kind of process.
You must do the 'hard yards' just as the athlete does.
They make sacrifices work and at their game constantly as they must.

To be truly professional you must do this too.
The athlete is totally focused, but that's a key to success (in anything).

Artists find certain media, colours, or subjects, interest them most.
Because of their focus, they get better at their specialty.
They apply knowledge and experience with greater depth and understanding.
BUT what you can't do is both specialize and not specialize.

As you should already know, it's not art skills that decide success.
Someone without these shouldn't be trying to build a professional career.
But many people do have those skills and are still not successful.
It's because they have no understanding the attitude necessary for success.

You create whatever you please in whatever way you want.
Once the work is created and you are happy, the creative process is over.
If desired the commercial process can then start.

The commercial part can start earlier and blend with a creative process.
Nothing indicates that making such a choice will mean a lesser quality work.
They are two different things when we discuss making art and selling.

Business principles apply to your commercial activities.
Artists are no different from - musicians, poets, accountants or hairdressers.
Provided they are involved in a commercial endeavour.

Commerce is not prejudiced to, or against, any particular sort of art.
If you want to sell you must use marketing ideas to market work effectively.

You produce whatever works you need to make the sales you desire.
If the works do the job your client wants, they do not have to be the best.
The humblest new car provides quite satisfactory service for most motorists.

It's possible to have a need to create and a need to sell, and to do both.
Without compromising either for that isn't a choice you have to make.

6. The toughest part is actually deciding what to do FIRST.

I had this problem once - I didn't know how to start a painting.
What I found out, and I suppose others have as well, it didn't actually matter!
Just as long as it was something.

Many people waste time working out the best thing to do.
Instead of starting and then turning that into the best thing they could.
That way procrastination also becomes a thing of the past!

People are exhorted to set goals so they can decide what to do.
This doesn't work if goal-setting becomes the activity.
You still have to get started.
It is better to do something without goals than spend time deciding goals.
Particularly if you do not actually do anything.

That's success secret #1: The ability to get started.
It's really no secret – just something that has to be done!
The biggest thing plaguing people struggling is an inability to get started.

People are stuck on trying to figure out the details of their career.
They research, prepare, make sure everything is "perfect" before starting!

It's totally unnecessary.
That's a way of putting it off for another day.
Usually that really means someone is scared!
Scared it's not going to work.
Scared you're going to look stupid.
Scared you might lose some money.
Scared you'll be judged.

So what if all that was GUARANTEED to happen?
Your friends will almost certainly judge you and talk behind your back.
They'll say what a fool you are for trying to make money as an artist.
At least one of them will believe you've fallen for a get-rich-quick scheme.

Stop worrying about it and get it out of the way!

Go ahead and power through it but hurry up so you can get to the good stuff. It's like gobbling vegetables when you were a kid so you could get dessert.

7. Just how serious are you?

What does a professional artist have to do?
It's a commitment - a doctor makes a similar one.

It's not easy!
It's lonely and hard – particularly at first but you need to be single-minded.
Be independent, you DON'T need other artists, or art knowledge.
You DO need business knowledge.

You are entirely responsible for your own success.
You are the only artist you have any control over.
Can you do all that?
How will it affect others (family, friends)?

You are a professional artist or you are not.
But if you decide, there's no looking back.
Be proud of your profession for it is a worthwhile and rewarding one.

Are you this committed?
Could you work for three to four days a week at a regular job?
Then finance and set up your own studio and art career the rest of the week?

There are some key aspects to make such an approach workable.
You must have determination and the job worked in must be tolerable.
There must be opportunities to work part time.
Financial reward from this should be sufficient to cover your career needs.

What about applying for grants and other forms of government assistance?
That path does not develop the strength of character which is necessary for any artist.

5. TIME MANAGEMENT.

Reviewed by Carol Stewart - (Wagga Wagga, Australia)

1. The start stops most people.
2. Procrastination is a waste of time.
3. Do you find you just can't find the time?
4. Are you organized?
5. Do you forget things?

1. The start stops most people.

Have you ever waited for inspiration?
Did you find that you had to wait for a long time?
Here's how I discovered how to avoid the start stopping me!

In my student days I arrived for an art class and was the only person!
Our lecturer for this class didn't ever have much to say, when he was there.
BUT often he wasn't there.
My fellow class members followed his pattern too, for this was a night class.
But I decided not to waste my time.

I looked at my blank canvas but didn't know what to do.
Have you had this feeling?
Yes the start certainly had me stopped - it was totally unexpected.

I was almost three quarters through a four year the course.
And I did not know what to do.
I now realize that teachers and lecturers provide the starting point.
Students are not usually in the situation that I found myself.

After a while, I looked at my paints, and noticed a tube of Indian Red.
If I was going to waste some paint it may as well be a colour I didn't like!
I still didn't know what to do though.
I mixed the Indian red with some turps, still with no real idea of what to do.

Then just because the paint was runny, I flicked some onto the canvas.
I splashed some more and still further splashes followed the first ones.
I looked at the canvas for a while, all covered with splashes of Indian red.
It was a bit like an Indian red 'Jackson Pollock' painting.

Still not knowing what to do, I decided to join the dots.
After a while the canvas was all covered with irregular shapes.
But I was no further ahead in working out what to do.

More speculation led me to the idea I could colour some of the shapes.
I squeezed out a small amount of white and blocked-in some of the shapes.
Then I used various white and Indian red mixtures.
Eventually I finished and had another look at what I had done.

Even though I didn't know what to do, I had done something.
It was an abstract painting which I had not anticipated that before starting.
But I was reasonably pleased with the result.

But even more importantly no longer did the start stop me.
I had found the solution to that particular artistic problem.

It doesn't matter what you do at the start, as long as you do something.
It can even be quite random.
That doesn't necessarily have to be the case though.

There is no need to wait for inspiration - just make a few marks.
That's what your mind needs to feed on.
Imagination cannot work on a blank surface, it needs help!
So whenever you feel artist's block, just do something, anything.
Then the start will not stop you.

Did you have this kind of experience in the seed experiment?

Saving time is no different - don't wait, just get on with it!
Get started and then your imagination can work for you!

2. Procrastination is a waste of time.

Doing something is better than nothing, even randomly, you can learn.
It doesn't matter what you do, the most important thing is to actually start.
Once you begin, alter or change what you've done, but something happens.

You can, and usually will, build on it.
Where you end up, won't be random (even if the start was).
It will also be considerably better than you could imagine in the beginning.

It's better to do something and be wrong, than do nothing.
We try to solve all our problems before we start and that's usually too hard.
Mistakes are fixed, or turned into something new, or you learn what not to do.

Your seed experiment was like this wasn't it?
Increasing experience and confidence as later starts improve on earlier ones.
But even then you must start.

That's why I also believe perfectionism is a waste of time.
Working things out along the way begins a path of continued improvement.
This will lead to highs never even imagined by the perfectionists.
This is also the Bill Gates (Microsoft) approach!
There really is no need to procrastinate on anything; it's just a waste of time.

A reason for this is once you act on an idea it is tested in the real world.
Your idea is held up and inspected.
It will stand or fail, or maybe even both, but in different ways.

You can then take further actions.
Modify what needs modifying, develop other areas that can be developed.
This is how an idea is improved and can be greater than the original thought.
Which otherwise would have remained as an untested idea.

Probably this also illustrates how life twists and turns.
Decisions based on superficial understandings can affect all that follows.
You really do owe it to yourself to weigh everything up, all the time.
In life there are always choices – just make them and then get on with it.

3. Do you find you just can't find the time?

How do you start your career -- or take it to the next level?
You must **MAKE TIME** to achieve goals or you're never going to reach them.
It's as simple as that so how do you do it - how do you find the time?
You're busy with everything else in your life as well as actually painting?

It's about how you set your goals.
The main reason people fail when they start a career is no clear direction.
They follow one idea after another with no clear path to success.
Not seeing anything to completion is why people fail once a business starts!
You'll **NEVER** achieve any success if you spend time going in all directions.
You simply can't chase every opportunity that comes your way.

Set goals with specific timelines for yourself.
Have carefully thought-out action plans to help you hit those goals.
You'll achieve success faster than you would have thought possible.

Ideally your goals should be measurable.
Instead of a goal like, "I want to be rich!" -- come up with a dollar value.
The amount you want to make in 3-5 years' time is a goal you should aim for.

Ask yourself in 3-5 years, what do you want your life to look like?
Consider finances **AND** what do you want your art business to be like then?

Think big -- but stay within reason!
Rome wasn't built in a day... or in five years, for that matter.

Set annual goals.
Break it into manageable objectives where you want to be in 3-5 years.

Let's take a look at what you want to achieve in the next year.
What do you need to do in the next 365 days to achieve your 3-5 year goals?
Write down as many goals as possible - you'll come up with a big list!

Then reduce that list down to the top 5 must-do items.
What are the top 5 things you **MUST** do to achieve your ultimate goals?
Once you answer this question, you'll have your top five goals for the year.

Set quarterly goals.
Those yearly goals still seem pretty big.
To achieve them, you must break them down into more realistic milestones.

Your quarterly goals you should do every three months.
That means you set quarterly goals for January, April, July, and October.

At the beginning of each quarter:
Take a step back - look at how well you managed your last quarterly goal.
Based on that, decide what you need to do during the next three months.
Then you'll keep moving toward those annual goals.

Set your monthly goals.
Decide the top 5 goals you have to achieve each month to hit quarterly goals.
But don't stop there set weekly goals.
What are the top things that must happen this week to hit the monthly goals?
Don't limit yourself to five weekly goals, sometimes there are less or more.

Set your daily goals.
Each morning, before checking emails - list things that have to happen today.
Once again, these tasks should drive you toward your weekly goals.
It doesn't matter if you have only an hour a day to spend on your career.
Set goals and focus on the really important things you need to achieve.
You'll be surprised how much you can accomplish in a short period of time.

But you still need to MAKE THE TIME.
If you spend only two hours a week on building or growing your business.
Once you have all your goals down on paper, don't file them away!
Make sure you can see them in a number of different places.

Tack them to the wall of your office or studio.
On a fridge - beside TV - beside a toilet, you need that constant reminder.

The only person holding you accountable for those goals is YOU.
Start setting those goals **NOW**.
Follow this system, in 30 days you'll surprise yourself at your progress!

The way to get anything done is just do it.
To get anything done you have to take a step, do something positive, begin.
It took three pages to write this simple concept (I do that sort of thing too).

To get a job done just do it but how do you just do it?
If you begin every day with a "to do" list then that is a start.
All tasks, large or small, are written down and given a priority.
Large jobs are broken down into smaller parts and reprioritized.
As the tasks are completed, they are marked off the list.
Put any leftovers on next day's list and give equal weight in prioritizing.
Eventually most things get done.
It is easy to prioritize using a computer to shift tasks around.

But your list has no value if you never can cross anything off.
To get things done you have to do them.

A list has things you don't have skills authority or materials to do?
You might as well cross them off because you can't do them.
They shouldn't be on your list.
Replace them with other tasks such as "Learn how to …" or "Assign to …"

But useful as the "to do" list is you shouldn't become a slave to the list.
If you are busy it is inevitable you will be interrupted during your working day.
Flexibility is needed to change directions and reorganize priorities.

It is also needed to solve immediate problems.
Move through your list at a somewhat regular pace as your day proceeds.
It is very basic and very simple - just do it!

4. Are you organized?

Most artists are nowhere near as well organized as they could be.
This means most people are nowhere near as efficient as they could be.

Space and time are the two basic ingredients of our universe.
One is infinite, but the other is not!
An interaction of the two creates change a fact of life most people say.

We tend to waste the finite ingredient, time.
Whatever time we have is limited so time wasted we never have again.
It makes a great deal of sense to use our time as wisely as possible.

Time management is clear objectives for day, week, a month, further.
Then you know what is important and what is not.

There's never enough time to do everything you want, and must do.
Are you the person who spends all your time fighting crocodiles?
BUT the real task is to drain the swamp?

That's why you need to differentiate between important and urgent.
Things, which are urgent, are not important to you – but important to others.
You manage these aspects by learning to say 'No, not no, but I can later.'
You'll never be successful until you learn this as people interrupt your studio.
The family is your worst enemy in this regard.

Do the important things first:
If you don't do this, they'll bank up and then you have a crisis on your hands.
Each day make up a list of things you must do and prioritize them.
Do the first and continue until you finish or can't do more, then do the next.

Urgent and important aren't necessarily the same.
Understand this difference is the key to effective time management.
The main thing is to do the important things first, so they don't bank up.
Most people tend to do the urgent things first.

Here's a matrix to illustrate the idea:

	URGENT	NOT URGENT
IMPORTANT	**1. Crises** Pressing problems, Deadlines, Major project True recreation.	**2.Preparation** Crisis prevention. Values clarification, Relationship building,
UNIMPORTANT	**3. Interruptions,** Some calls, mail, Some reports, Some meetings, Many popular activities.	**4.Trivia,** Some mail, time wasters, Some phone calls, Many pleasant activities. Busywork.

What makes a professional career successful?
You MUST pay attention to Box 2 because that's your FUTURE!
Forget those areas and your future will be the same as the present situation.
That's why success of any business is in 2. IMPORTANT but NOT URGENT.
There's a tendency to put off those things.

It almost goes without saying; we do the things required in Box 1.
There's also a tendency to do too much of Box 3.
The URGENT but UNIMPORTANT can be put off until later, but often isn't.
Usually these things are urgent for other people but not yourself.
Box 4, UNIMPORTANT and NOT URGENT, often need not be done at all.

Success is linked to how well you do <u>important but not urgent</u> things.

5. Do you forget things?

A common time management idea is to use 'To Do' Lists.
Just make lists of things you have to do - on paper or in the computer.
They help prioritize tasks - I do a weekly one, but if life is hectic, do this daily.

Write a to-do-list every day.
The most important technique in time management is setting priorities.
Decide daily the most important, so you know how to spend your time wisely.
Take a few minutes at the start of each day.
Just write down what you need to accomplish.
Then rank every item to show its priority.

That way you have a plan for the day.
It's even better to do this at the end of each day.

Write down what you need to do to-morrow.
Make a habit of doing your list before leaving the studio each day.
If this is not possible, or if you work at home, do it at night for the next day.

Using this process you can sleep on the actions required.
Many problems will solve themselves overnight.

Highlight the priority items.
The matrix above will give you an idea about what to do.
Obviously the IMPORTANT and URGENT area will contain the priority items.
Don't forget about Box 2 though.
Put some of these into your To Do List each day.

At the end of the day, cross out the items which have been completed.
Then make a new list for the next day so your priorities are clearly focused.

On the last day of your week:
Review the lists for that week.
If one issue keeps coming up, then either drop it or deal with it!

Set deadlines.
Do similar tasks at the same time.
For example do all your phone calls in one time-block.
But in another time period you might attend to your correspondence.
Of course you'll need to plan your painting time too.
This approach to time allocation means you focus better and more efficiently.

Learn to say no.
Concentrate on completing your own work before doing what others want.

Are you a morning, afternoon or evening person?
Schedule your most important activities in your prime time.

Don't waste time on the Internet!
Only some of you would do that.

Don't disappear under written material.
Read something, file it then or throw it away.

Learn to delegate.
I mean really delegate.
Actually let the other person do whatever it is.

Don't be afraid to skip meetings.
Many are not worth attending except for social reasons.

Exercising also saves time.
You'll be more alert and make better use of your time if you are fit.
Eat properly too.

6. MOVING AHEAD.

Reviewed by Ebigbagha Sylvester – (Wilberforce Island, Nigeria.)

    1. Let's put the seed experiment to some use!

    2. Increase productivity - work a number of paintings.

    3. Use your 200+ experiments to explore variations.

1. Let's put the seed experiment to some use!

Whenever you feel artist's block, just do something, anything.
Small experiments avoid any preciousness being attached to a result.
So keep this exercise to about 35cm x 25cm or **LESS**.

It doesn't matter what you do at the start, as long as you do something.
It can even be quite random, as my first self-discovered starts were.
There is no need to wait for inspiration - a few marks is all your mind needs.
Imagination cannot work on a blank surface, it needs help!
Eventually random starts do not necessarily have to be the case.

Do this regularly, even daily.
Make 5 or 10 or 20 experiments a part of your daily routine.
Now paint 200 or more (250 or even 300) of these small experiments.
The quality improves, particularly if you don't worry about it when painting.
Naturally this improvement will not be at the start.
It will take some time before you notice the improvement, but it WILL happen!

Enjoy a no pressure attitude, with pleasing results from time to time.
Small sizes will speed up production of those 200+ experiments.
Your 200 or more experiments are mainly to develop your ability and attitude.
You'll not be concerned with sales because that puts pressure on.
You become careful and that slows the process down.

Framing 200 small works costs money so don't frame them.
If they aren't to be framed or sold it will not matter if they turn well out or not.

Also don't worry about having proper stretchers and the best materials.
Save that for when your art career really gets under way.
Cut boards from craftwood or ply in two or three different sizes.
Glue canvas to them if you wish to prepare panels and away you go.
Even paint on paper or cardboard - it won't matter what you paint on!

What will become of all those experimental paintings?
Nothing, but save them if you like, even the ones that didn't work out.
Professional artists needs a detached view of their work so develop that!

2. Increase productivity - work a number of paintings at the same time.

Once you run into a dead-end with one painting go to another.
Eliminate waste time and most works finish fresh and about the same time.

Eventually the initial painting is returned to.
Maybe you can't remember what you were doing previously on a work?
Just get going with whatever you can think of now for it doesn't matter!

Working on a number of paintings at the same time saves materials.
A particular colour can be applied to the work for which it was intended.
There are bound to be other works where that colour will be appropriate.
Right now we are looking for improvement and consistency.
The 200+ exercises is pre-season training, to use a sporting analogy.

Not all of the exercises will turn out perfectly.
But that won't matter because you'll learn a great deal from the 'failures'.
You'll learn what to do and what not to do next time.

You are the judge of quality, which is a variable that changes over time.
You have old works you thought were excellent at the time they were done.

What are they like now?
There will be major works of a standard you can be truly proud of.

Another way to speed up your painting is to use larger brushes.
Try various brushes and see how large a brush you can use.
With practice you can paint most of any painting with a large brush or two.
House painting brushes can be used instead of artists' brushes.
If necessary, finer brushes can be used to finish off the work.

If you are passionate then anything you do has that quality.
So do not worry about matters like that, for they look after themselves.
Maintaining motivation and enthusiasm is more related to why you paint.

Right now you'll have to avoid major works though.

You'll tend to labour over them as you seek to do your best.

They take time are usually done slowly and are usually large and complex.

3. Use your 200+ experiments to explore variations.

Vary subjects, styles, colours, or whatever you feel the need to explore.
There's no pressure to do this, but no reason not to either.
One experiment leads to the next, and five or six more, so explore variations.

Let's say you want to learn to paint the human figure?
Then put figures in your daily experiments.
Do not worry how they turn out just paint them and in time they'll improve.

There's nothing to be anxious about.
They are not for sale, show, framing but experiments to explore thoughts.
Just get on and do them without worrying about how they turn out.

Skill comes from practice, style comes from within.
An exhibition that look as if there are several different artists.
Show a lack of style but possibly a mastery of skill.
Where all the works look the same or similar show the artist's style.
You may like it or not, but it's there (e.g. van Gogh).

One artist reported getting off track with her experiments.
She'd been experimenting but working bigger than had been suggested.

She had only done about 22 experiments.
Six of those weren't much good so they were painted over or discarded.
BUT painting over discarded works, actually counts as new paintings!
She could also cut up some of those big paintings and paint over them too.

Experimenting is fine but working bigger is not.
That just takes extra time for no advantage.
You use more materials and tend to do "a painting" instead of experimenting.

This artist has fallen into that trap.
If she thought of the paintings as experiments.
Then she wouldn't care about six being not so good.

That's part of the deal.
You can learn from those too.

OK she hasn't followed the experimental approach very accurately.
She is painting so that's a start and is more important than she follow exactly.
Now she needs to develop a focus to what she does.
That can come via many small experiments.

Doing many small studies is a process of finding out how they turn out.
It's a discovery process rather than producing something.
Sometimes they'll turn out great, but at other times not so.

So regard these paintings as exercises or studies.
They are never going to be framed, sold or kept for posterity.
The main aim is to do a lot and do them reasonably quickly.
So shut your eyes and have a go!

You don't need to be brave for there is no risk.
Many artists are too careful!
They are frightened of making a mistake.
There's no such thing, only something you learn.

If you fear mistakes you'll never learn anything.
You'll only repeat what you already know.
Just enjoy the painting.

You learn to paint by painting, (just like the boy who did budgerigars).
There's nothing that beats "brush mileage" as a way of learning to paint.
You do not learn by someone telling you what to do.
You only learn they know what to do and if you get stuck you can ask them.

WHERE NEXT:

BUT being a professional artist is NOW harder than it ever was.
There are other books that link with this book.
You might need one or more of them:

PRICE RIGHT - Then sell.
http://www.amazon.com/dp/B087S85HS8

PLANNING - Means success.
http://www.amazon.com/dp/B087SCD1NY

CAREER BASICS - Planning.
http://www.amazon.com/dp/B087SCJYX3

FINDING BUYERS - How?
http://www.amazon.com/dp/B087SM58GJ

FIRST WEBSITE - Simple is best.
http://www.amazon.com/dp/B087SFZ6RD

SUCCESSFUL SELLING - Learn how.
http://www.amazon.com/dp/B087SHDKPN

FRAMING = helps sales
http://www.amazon.com/dp/B087SGS6MB

CHRISTMAS - Special approaches.
http://www.amazon.com/dp/B087SHDKPN

TAKE THE PLUNGE - become professional
http://www.amazon.com/dp/B087SFTD61

COPYRIGHT - make money from copyright.
http://www.amazon.com/dp/B0892HWYTV

NOT NOW:

Perhaps one of these books could interest you?

Write about your own memories.
http://www.amazon.com/dp/B087DWKPTP

A simple way to start developing creativity.
If you are a parent, teacher or someone who meets a group regularly?
http://www.amazon.com/dp/B088T1KFQZ

Here is how most people start becoming an artist!
http://www.amazon.com/dp/B088Y1DPL6

Here are some of my own memories.
http://www.amazon.com/dp/B088Y4RPL9

Start an art career but it's **NOW** is harder than it ever was.
http://www.amazon.com/dp/B088T7VJ76

SEND TO:

Know anyone interested in chocolate recipes? Then send them this link.

http://www.amazon.com/dp/B088Y4RPL9

Know anyone interested in THIS book?

http://www.amazon.com/dp/B087S87HLD